NEW YORK TRAVEL PICTU

AN EDUCATIONAL COUNTRY TRAVEL PICTURE BOOK FOR KIDS ABOUT USA HISTORY, DESTINATION PLACES, ANIMALS AND MANY MORE

New York

Copyright ©2024 James K. Mahi

All rights reserved

New York State is nicknamed the "Empire State."

What is the capital city of New York State?

The capital city of New York State is Albany.

When did New York become a state?

July 26, 1788

What is a major industry in New York State besides finance?

Agriculture – apples, grapes, dairy

What natural wonder is located on the border between New York State and Canada?

Niagara Falls, a famous waterfall, is located on the border between New York State and Canada.

New York City is known for its diverse population. How many languages are spoken there?

Over 800 languages

Bordered by how many Great Lakes is New York State?

Two – Lake Erie and Lake Ontario

Besides the Statue of Liberty, what other cool statue is in New York?

There's a giant bronze bull on Wall Street charging right ahead. It's called the Charging Bull, and it's a symbol of strength and determination!

When you see a big, beautiful orange butterfly in New York, what might it be?

That could be a monarch butterfly, and New York is an important stop on their long migration journey!

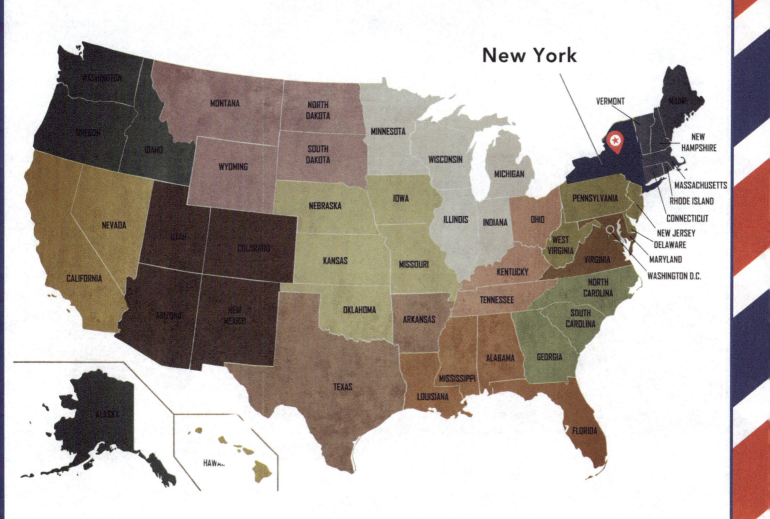

The United States is the fourth largest country in the world, after Russia, Canada, and China.

New York is the 27th largest state in the United States by area.

New York City is the largest city in the state and the most populous city in the country.

The state motto of New York is "Excelsior," which means "Ever Upward" in Latin.

The New York State bird is the Eastern Bluebird.

The Erie Canal, completed in 1825, played a significant role in the state's economic development.

The Adirondack Park in upstate New York is the largest publicly protected area in the contiguous United States.

New York City's Central Park is one of the most visited urban parks in the world.

The Statue of Liberty, a symbol of freedom and democracy, stands on Liberty Island in New York Harbor.

The Finger Lakes region in upstate New York is famous for its numerous glacial lakes.

The New York Stock Exchange on Wall Street is one of the largest stock exchanges in the world.

The Catskill Mountains in southeastern New York are known for their scenic beauty and outdoor recreational opportunities.

The Hudson River, running through eastern New York, played a crucial role in the state's early exploration and commerce.

New York City's Times Square is famous for its bright lights, Broadway shows, and New Year's Eve celebrations.

The Adirondack Mountains contain over 2,000 miles of hiking trails.

The Tappan Zee Bridge, spanning the Hudson River, connects Rockland and Westchester counties.

The state of New York is named after the Duke of York, who later became King James II of England.

New York City's subway system is one of the oldest and largest in the world.

The "Big Apple" is a nickname for New York City that originated in the 1920s.

The state tree of New York is the Sugar Maple.

Lake Ontario, one of the Great Lakes, forms part of New York's northern border with Canada.

New York City's Chinatown is one of the largest Chinese communities outside of Asia.

The New York Botanical Garden in the Bronx is one of the largest botanical gardens in the world.

The New York State Museum in Albany features exhibits on the state's natural and cultural history.

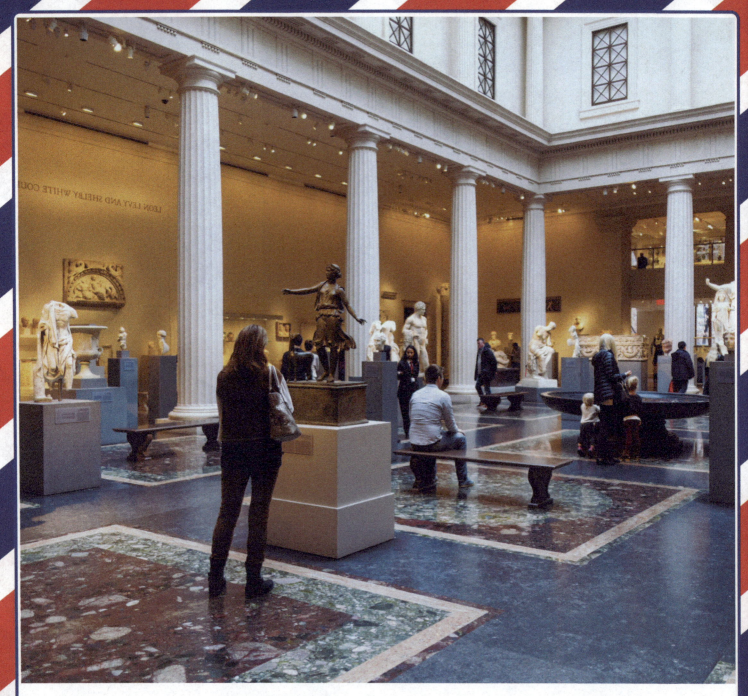

New York City's Metropolitan Museum of Art is one of the largest and most prestigious art museums in the world.

The Thousand Islands region, located along the St. Lawrence River, is famous for its picturesque scenery and summer resorts.

The Appalachian Trail, one of the longest hiking trails in the world, passes through New York's Hudson Valley.

The Brooklyn Bridge, completed in 1883, was the longest suspension bridge in the world at the time of its construction.

The United Nations headquarters is located in New York City.

The New York State Thruway is one of the longest toll roads in the United States.

New York City's Empire State Building was the tallest building in the world when it was completed in 1931.

The New York State Fairgrounds in Syracuse hosts various events throughout the year, including concerts and festivals.

The New York State Department of Environmental Conservation oversees the protection and management of natural resources in the state.

New York City's Rockefeller Center is famous for its art deco architecture and ice skating rink.

Lake Placid, located in the Adirondack Mountains, hosted the Winter Olympics in 1932 and 1980.

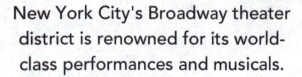

New York City's Broadway theater district is renowned for its world-class performances and musicals.

The Hudson Valley is renowned for its historic estates and scenic beauty.

The state gem of New York is the Garnet.

The state insect of New York is the Nine-Spotted Ladybug.

The New York Public Library is one of the largest public library systems in the world.

The "I Love New York" slogan was created in 1977 to promote tourism in the state.

The New York City Marathon is one of the largest and most prestigious marathons in the world.

The state fish of New York is the Brook Trout.

The New York State Department of Environmental Conservation oversees the protection and management of natural resources in the state.

The New York City skyline features iconic skyscrapers such as the Chrysler Building and One World Trade Center.

Ellis Island, located near the Statue of Liberty, was the main entry point for immigrants to the United States from 1892 to 1954.

Explore New York State: Travel Tips for an Unforgettable Adventure

1. **Plan ahead:** Before your trip, research places you want to visit and make a rough itinerary.
2. **Pack for the weather:** Check the weather forecast and pack appropriate clothing and gear.
3. **Bring comfortable shoes:** New York State has a lot of walking and hiking opportunities, so bring comfortable shoes.
4. **Explore public transportation:** New York City has a great subway system, and other cities have buses and trains. It can be an easy and affordable way to get around.
5. **Try local food:** New York State is famous for its diverse cuisine, so don't miss out on trying local dishes like New York-style pizza or bagels.
6. **Visit iconic landmarks:** Don't forget to visit famous landmarks like the Statue of Liberty, Times Square, and Central Park.
7. **Explore beyond the city:** New York State has beautiful natural areas like the Adirondack Mountains and the Finger Lakes region. Consider taking a day trip to explore nature.
8. **Be respectful:** Remember to be respectful of local customs and cultures, and always follow rules and regulations.
9. **Stay safe:** Keep your belongings secure, especially in crowded tourist areas, and be aware of your surroundings.
10. **Have fun:** Enjoy your trip to New York State and make lots of memories!

EXPLORING INTERESTING USA FACTS

The United States is made up of 50 states.

The American flag has 50 stars, each representing a state.

The Statue of Liberty was a gift from France to the United States in 1886.

The tallest mountain in the United States is Mount Denali in Alaska.

The Grand Canyon in Arizona is one of the world's most famous natural wonders.

The United States is home to the world's largest economy.

The United States is known as the "melting pot" because people from many different countries live there.

The United States celebrates Independence Day on July 4th to mark the signing of the Declaration of Independence in 1776.

New York City is the largest city in the United States.

The American bald eagle is the national bird of the United States.

NASA sends astronauts to space from the Kennedy Space Center in Florida.

The Mississippi River is the longest river in the United States.

The United States has more national parks than any other country.

The Liberty Bell in Philadelphia, Pennsylvania, is a symbol of American independence.

The United States has the world's largest military.

The United States is known for its diverse landscapes, including mountains, deserts, forests, and beaches.

The United States is the birthplace of famous inventions like the light bulb, the telephone, and the internet.

The American automotive industry produces millions of cars each year.

Hawaii is the only U.S. state made up entirely of islands.

The United States has the world's largest collection of museums, including the Smithsonian Institution in Washington, D.C.

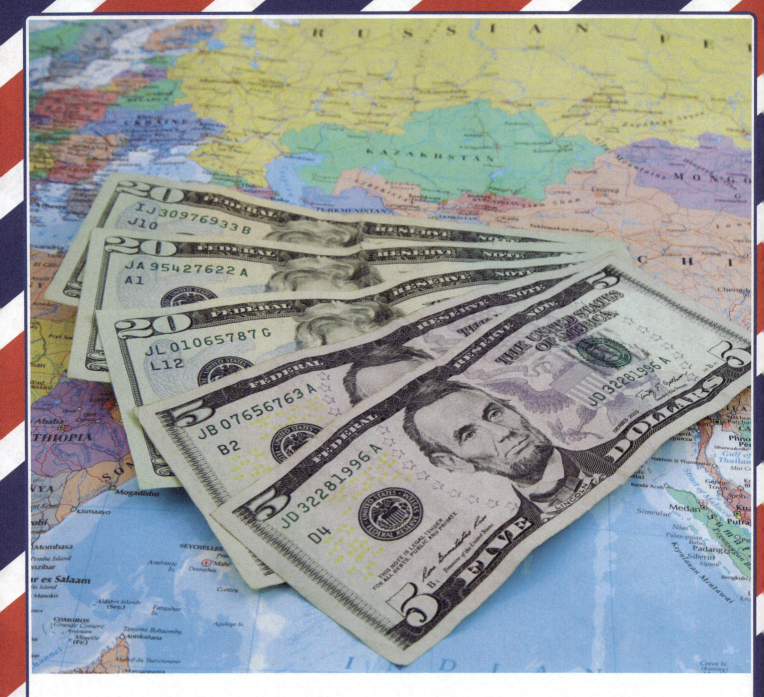

The U.S. dollar is the world's primary reserve currency, meaning it is widely used in international transactions.

The United States has more Nobel Prize winners than any other country.

NASA's Apollo 11 mission successfully landed the first humans on the moon in 1969.

The U.S. Interstate Highway System is one of the largest networks of highways in the world, spanning over 46,000 miles.

The Smithsonian National Air and Space Museum in Washington, D.C., houses the Wright brothers' original airplane, the Wright Flyer.

The United States has the world's largest economy, with a Gross Domestic Product (GDP) exceeding $28 trillion.

Florida - Miami is a popular beach destination with a vibrant nightlife scene and a strong Latin American influence.

Los Angeles, California - LA is the heart of the American film industry and is home to Hollywood.

Yellowstone National Park is the oldest national park in the USA

The President of the United States lives and works in the White House in Washington, D.C.

Delaware is the first state to ratify the U.S. Constitution and is known for its tax-free shopping.

New Jersey is famous for its boardwalks, Atlantic City casinos, and proximity to New York City.

10 FASCINATING LESS KNOWN FACTS ABOUT THE USA

- The United States has the world's longest cave system, Mammoth Cave in Kentucky, stretching over 400 miles underground.
- The Great Stalacpipe Organ, located in Luray Caverns, Virginia, is the world's largest musical instrument and plays music by tapping on stalactites.
- The Library of Congress in Washington, D.C., is the largest library in the world, with over 168 million items in its collections.
- The shortest street in the United States is McKinley Street in Bellefontaine, Ohio, measuring only 20 feet long.
- The Empire State Building in New York City has its own zip code, 10118, and its own postal address.
- The United States has the world's largest ball of twine, located in Cawker City, Kansas, with a circumference of over 40 feet.
- The Hawaiian alphabet has only 13 letters: A, E, I, O, U, H, K, L, M, N, P, W, and a symbol called an 'okina ('), representing a glottal stop.
- The U.S. state of Wyoming has more antelope than people, with an estimated population of over 500,000 antelope.
- The world's first ever motel, the Motel Inn, opened in San Luis Obispo, California, in 1925.
- The city of Juneau, Alaska, is the only U.S. state capital that is not accessible by road; it can only be reached by boat or plane due to its location in a mountainous region.

Made in the USA
Coppell, TX
03 August 2024